COLLECTING INFORMATION FOR SCHOOL IMPROVEMENT

Model questionnaires and research instruments

John Beresford

With a foreword by Professor David Hopkins

David Fulton Publishers
London

David Fulton Publishers Ltd
Ormond House, 26–27 Boswell Street, London WC1N 3JD

First published in Great Britain by David Fulton Publishers 1998

Note: The right of John Beresford to be identified as the author of this work has been asserted by him in accordance with the Copyright, Designs and Patents Act 1988.

Copyright © John Beresford 1998

British Library Cataloguing in Publication Data
A catalogue record for this book is available from the British Library

ISBN 1–85346–556–9

Typeset by Textype Typesetters Ltd, Cambridge
Printed in Great Britain by Hobbs the Printers Ltd, Totton, Hampshire

Contents

Foreword

As John Beresford notes in his Introduction, the 'Improving the Quality of Education For All' school improvement project began in Cambridge in the early 1990s. The overall aim of the project is to strengthen the school's capacity to provide quality education for all its pupils by building upon existing good practice, research evidence of effective practices and the use of high quality diagnostic data. In so doing, the IQEA team are also producing and evaluating a model of school development, and are using the opportunity of collaboration with schools in the IQEA network to conduct a long-term investigation into the processes of school change and student achievement.

From the outset, the IQEA project was conceived of as a research and development project committed both to supporting and understanding the process of change and development in schools. The nature of our research and development work within the IQEA project is inevitably iterative. We engage in research and theory-building by reviewing the knowledge base, gathering data, reflecting on outcomes, formulating hypotheses, testing them out, and refining them – all in collaboration with schools in the network.

One of the recent key findings of recent research on school effectiveness and school improvement is that any school improvement strategy needs to be 'context specific'. They need to be built on high quality information about the current state of the school. Data provide a fundamental foundation for school improvement strategies and provide energy and direction for change.

During this programme of research and development into school improvement we have come to recognise that teachers are extremely interested in data relating to their own schools, and are prepared to take part in the collection of that data. While we have found the more traditional research methods such as interviews, questionnaires and observations to be useful in such collection, we have felt that there is room for new, user-friendly yet penetrating techniques for investigating and measuring the complex processes and relationships involved in school change. It is because we found only limited methodological guidance in the existing research literature that Mel Ainscow, David Hargreaves and I developed six new techniques for mapping the process of change in schools. A comprehensive description of the techniques, with advice on administration, is found in the manual produced as a result of the research, *Mapping Change in Schools: the Cambridge Manual of Research Techniques* (Cambridge University 1994).

The mapping approach is a way of developing research techniques which capture the perspectives of those involved in the change process in organisations such as schools. These techniques were to be more efficient for the researcher, more interesting for the subject and more penetrating in terms of the quality of data than was possible in the most commonly used techniques in the field.

The development of techniques both for research and staff development is characteristic of the IQEA approach to school improvement. Uniform with this volume, for example, are our two Handbooks on the 'School Level Conditions' (Ainscow *et al.* 1994) and 'Classroom Level Conditions' (Hopkins *et al.* 1997). These books evolved from our early realisation that school change efforts that failed to focus on the internal conditions of schools and their management arrangements, as well as on the primary target of curriculum and pedagogic change, were soon marginalised.

Collecting Information for School Improvement provides very specific information on which to base a school improvement strategy. Many of the schools in which we have worked recently have found the range of instruments contained in this handbook helpful, not only in gathering data but in sharply focusing their classroom development interventions.

John Beresford is to be congratulated not only for gathering these instruments together but also for the assiduous work he has done over the years in IQEA schools and classrooms in gathering information about student learning. I hope that, through the publication of this handbook, many other schools will have the opportunity to use these instruments to focus their school improvement effort on student learning – and in so doing to 'improve the quality of education for all'.

David Hopkins
School of Education
University of Nottingham
January 1998

References

Ainscow, M., Hopkins, D., Southworth, G. and West, M. (1994) *Creating the Conditions for School Improvement*. London: David Fulton Publishers.

Hopkins, D., West, M., Ainscow, M., Harris, A. and Beresford, J. (1997) *Creating the Conditions for Classroom Improvement*. London: David Fulton Publishers.

Introduction

The 1988 Education Act gave schools the power to plan for the most effective use of the limited amount of resources available to them. The activity generated by this empowerment has given rise, in effect, to the School Improvement and School Effectiveness movements. Schools have become increasingly interested in exploring different ways of deploying staff, staff expertise and budgets to the greatest effect in the delivery of the National Curriculum. Parents have become increasingly interested in schools' examination results. OFSTED inspectors use highly specific effectiveness criteria in assessing schools.

The interest of the school community in being effective has brought about a welcome and renewed interest in effective teaching and learning. The IQEA (Improving the Quality of Education for All) Project started in the early 1990s with a group of like-minded schools in the south of England exploring with tutors from the Cambridge Institute of Education ways of making teaching and learning more effective in their schools. How the project functioned is described in detail elsewhere (see Hopkins *et al.* 1994). The basic tenet of the project is that the internal conditions of the school have to be developed in order that the capacity of the school to self-improve can be established. While schools worked on developing this capacity they tackled various improvement projects under the guidance of the Cambridge tutors.

As well as reading research related to their school's improvement focus, teachers in the project were encouraged to collect and analyse data from their own school environment. To help in this I was fortunate enough to be appointed as Research Officer to the Cambridge-based project in October 1994. The project quickly spread, and IQEA outpost projects were established in Humberside and South Yorkshire. Since 1994 further IQEA-type projects have been set up in Hampshire, Nottinghamshire, Derbyshire, Iceland and Puerto Rico.

As well as the Cambridge project, I have also worked in Humberside and, more recently, in Derbyshire and Nottinghamshire. My job has been to help teachers to collect data, to help them analyse it and to liaise with tutors about the advice and guidance given to schools on the basis of the research. I have provided schools with literature relevant to their projects, and have provided coaching in research techniques. Part of our capacity-building is to enable schools to undertake their own research, so I am, in effect, striving to make myself redundant from the moment I enter a school.

Inevitably, similar schools choose similar areas for improvement. I have been able to use various observation and interview schedules on a number of occasions, because schools all over the country are concerned about issues such as classroom order, pupil motivation and self-esteem, independent learning and preferred teaching and learning styles. I have been privileged to work with teachers in over 40 schools, and in the three years I have been working for IQEA have interviewed and observed scores of teachers and literally hundreds of students. It was David Hopkins who suggested that I publish some of the more regularly-used techniques in a form which could be used independently by schools.

It is not every school which can afford the services of an external researcher. Almost all of the techniques in this book can, however, be used by teachers, by ancillary staff or even by cooperative parents. One of our project schools is training sixth formers in research techniques in order that they can undertake school-based research.

Schedules in this book have generally been tailored to the needs of individual schools. The language used in them often means they are Primary- or Secondary-specific. However, with careful rewriting or judicious revamping I am sure that most of them can be adjusted to the particular needs and circumstances in your school.

Each schedule is preceded by notes on the purpose of the instrument, advice on its administration and some comments on my own findings using the technique. I would like to thank the teachers, too many to name, who have worked with me on the production of many of the instruments in this book, as well as the guiding hands of Mel West at Cambridge and David Hopkins at Nottingham. The wit of one and the encouragement of the other have proved a stimulating combination. I hope you have as much pleasure using the techniques as I have.

John Beresford
Schools of Education
Universities of Cambridge and Nottingham
March 1998

Reference

Hopkins, D., Ainscow, M., West, M. (1994) *School Improvement in an Era of Change*. London, New York: Cassell.

General note

Many of the instruments following in this book are interview schedules. While it is possible to use a tape-recorder, I tend to favour note taking for the recording of data. The reasons for this are as follows:

- transcribing from tapes is a time-consuming and specialist activity. I do far too many interviews in a short space of time, and have to meet too many reporting deadlines, to put at risk my cordial relations with the secretariat at the universities of Cambridge and Nottingham;

- the sensitivity of much of the subject matter of school-based interviews, and assurances of anonymity given before interviews, mean that the storage and disposal of tapes become problematical. Teachers in particular seem happier and more forthright when notes are being taken than when tapes are being made.

Pupil adjustment to school

Introduction

Most teachers are rightly concerned about how well students adjust to the systems and mores of their school. Lack of adjustment can manifest itself in a number of ways – poor discipline, classroom disruption, student underachievement.

A number of our project schools have suffered from some of these, and have been concerned to find out why such breakdowns have occurred. Areas of enquiry have included:

- relationships with teachers;
- relations with other students;
- student self-esteem;
- perceived opportunities for independent learning;
- student aspirations;
- parental aspirations for students.

Contents of section

Interview schedule on pupils' learning histories

Interview schedule for Y7 and Y9 pupils on the school's culture

Interview schedule on pupils' attitudes to learning

Pupil interview schedule B on the learning culture

Staff interview schedule on the learning culture

Interview schedule on pupils' learning histories

Purpose of instrument

- to assess students' levels of self-esteem;
- to assess how well students have adjusted to school life.

Advice on administration

Although this can be used for all age groups from Year 3 to Year 13, it is ideally suited to assessing to what extent Year 7 students have integrated into the ways of secondary school. The schedule can be administered in quite large groups of up to six students, as long as the interviewer ensures that each student has a turn in answering each question. Groups can be of single or mixed gender. For purposes of assessing students' levels of self-esteem it is possible to interview students in ability groups chosen by staff.

Interviews, depending on the size of the group, can take between 15 and 30 minutes. They should take place in a quiet and, if the group is large, a fairly spacious area where the interviews are unlikely to be disturbed and where possible noise from the interview room will not disturb others. Students will give more authentic answers if the interviewer is not known to them, so a teacher who does not teach their classes, an ancillary or a parent could be used.

Some comments on findings

Year 7 students are not usually critical of their new school, so any criticisms need to be noted, particularly if they are regularly mentioned. Students who have adjusted well to school have fond early memories involving achievement, be it winning races or learning to read. Those who have adjusted less well tend to recall incidents involving perceived injustices wrought by fellow-students or teachers.

Interview schedule on pupils' learning histories

Year: **Gender:**

1. How would you describe your ability in school?

2. What makes you say that?

3. How long have you been like this?

4. What changed you?

5. What is your earliest memory of school?

6. What is your fondest memory of school?

7. What is your worst memory of school?

8. What did you like in your last school that doesn't exist/happen here?

9. What do you like here that wasn't at your last school?

Interview schedule for Y7 and Y9 pupils on the school's culture

Purpose of instrument

- to identify students' areas of concern relating to the organisational arrangements of secondary school;

- to explore students' views about the quality of relationships with secondary teachers compared to those they had with primary teachers;

- to identify the qualities of teachers with whom the students have a good relationship.

Advice on administration

Interviewing in single-sex groups of three ensures that everyone in the group has a say. A room where there is no likelihood of being disturbed is essential. The interviews should take about 20 minutes, allowing for about 15 groups to be interviewed during the average school day.

Students will not give authentic views about teachers unless they are guaranteed complete anonymity. This means that it would be difficult for a teaching member of staff to administer this particular interview. It could, however, be administered by a well-liked and trusted ancillary, or by a parent who is not known to the particular students being interviewed.

Some comments on findings

Students tend to be frank and incisive about their school and their teachers when they feel they can trust the interviewer. The comments of staff when students' views are fedback anonymously suggest that such views are generally just and fair.

Year 7 students are generally overwhelmed by the novelty of secondary school, and where they are happy they are largely uncritical. Where there are some difficulties of adjustment to the new environment then some criticism will emerge. Strictness of staff, bullying by older students and excessive homework are the most commonly cited.

Interview schedule for Y7 and Y9 pupils on the school's culture

1. Is secondary school different from your primary school?
   In what way?

2. Are secondary school-teachers different from primary school-teachers?
   In what way?

3. Have you one teacher you particularly get on with?
   What is it about him or her that you like?

4. Is it important to you where you sit in class?
   Why?

5. What do you particularly like about this school?

6. What would you change if you had the chance?

Interview schedule on pupils' attitudes to learning

Purpose of instrument

- to determine students' attitudes towards work in school;
- to determine students' views on working independently;
- to assess the aspirations of students, and of their parents for them;
- to assess what motivates, and demotivates, students in school.

Advice on administration

This schedule can be administered to any secondary year-group or, indeed, ability group. Again, single-sex groups of three are best for involving all students. This particular interview can take up to 25 minutes. A quiet room away from the main activities of the school day is an ideal setting.

Because students are being asked to make judgements about their own work performance as well as for their opinions about teaching and learning in the school, this interview would be best administered by someone unknown to the students.

Some comments on findings

Students vary in their attitude to secondary school largely according to which year they are in, and to their general orientation towards learning. Year 7 students are usually enthusiastic about their new school, an enthusiasm which recedes towards the end of Year 8. Social relationships now become important, and the academic demands of school begin to impinge upon these in Year 9. How students respond to this particular dilemma is an important determinant of attitudes towards school in this particular year.

Year 10 sees the start of GCSE examination courses, and a resignedness, often resentful, among most students that the work has to be done. Those students who in Year 9 were unable or unwilling to reconcile the demands of school and social life now face difficulties, and these often manifest themselves in disruptive behaviour. The resigned majority tend to shun them.

All students stress the importance of a meaningful relationship with at least one member of staff. Qualities associated with such a teacher include a sense of humour, understanding, approachability and a willingness to give time to the student to explain work.

Interview schedule on pupils' attitudes to learning

1. Do you like school?
   Why? (Why not?)

2. Is everything you do in school worthwhile?
   (Which parts aren't?)

3. What do you want to do when you leave school?

4. What do your parents want you to do?

5. How much homework do you do most evenings, on average?
   Is that more than/less than/the same as your friends?

6. Would you say you worked hard in school?
   (How do you know?)

7. Do you get chances to organise your own learning?
   (Would you like some/more?)

8. Describe a good lesson you've had recently.
   How did it begin?
   What happened during the lesson?
   How did it end?

9. Describe a bad lesson.

10. Without naming him/her, describe your favourite teacher in the school.
    What makes him/her a good teacher?

11. Is there anything the school could do to make learning easier for you (e.g. opportunities to catch up, different teaching methods)?

Pupil interview schedule B on the learning culture

Purpose of instrument

- to determine students' views on the administrative arrangements of the school;

- to assess the level of students' self-esteem;

√ - to identify key factors in changing students' attitudes to school and work.

Advice on administration

This schedule is best administered to different ability groupings identified by staff. This enables the levels of self-esteem of different groupings to be assessed. Groups of three are best, and can be of mixed or single gender. The interviews take about 20 minutes, so about 15 groups can be accommodated in a school day. A quiet room where disturbances are unlikely is best.

Older students may be willing to discuss their working habits frankly with members of staff who do not teach them. Younger students are less likely to be so frank, and would best be interviewed by someone who does not know them.

Some comments on findings

For comments on students' attitudes to school arrangements, see the notes on earlier schedules in this section. Sixth formers often rediscover the enthusiasm they showed in Year 7 for the facilities offered by the school, and are generally appreciative of any quality teaching they receive. Friendships with staff and other students are now well established.

Able students are generally more confident of their ability than those students identified by staff as average or less able. Students often cite the influence of a particular teacher, the identification of a learning difficulty or the mastery of reading as important factors in shaping their attitude towards work.

Pupil interview schedule B on the learning culture

1. What do you like about this school?

2. What do you dislike?

3. Do you have enough say in how the school is run?

4. In which kind of lessons do you learn well?

5. In which kind don't you learn?

6. How would you describe your ability?

7. Do you work hard?

8. Do your teachers' views of your ability match yours?

9. Have you always been like this?
   When, if ever, did you change?
   What made you change?

10. What do you think of homework?

11. What would you change about the school if you had the chance?

12. Is school important?
    Why? Why not?

Staff interview schedule on the learning culture

Purpose of instrument

- to feedback, and seek comments on, student views about the school;
- to seek staff's views about the school;
- to match staff's views with students' views.

Advice on administration

This particular schedule can be made specific to a particular subject area, and is therefore best administered to single members of staff. Absolute anonymity needs to be assured, and given the sensitivity of some of the questions it is best administered by someone from outside the school's community. The interview needs to take place in a room away from the daily business of school. Interviews can take up to 35 minutes, so about 12 are possible in a school day. Staff are, for various reasons, more able than students (and often more willing) to be interviewed after school has ended.

Some comments on findings

Where teachers can be guaranteed absolute anonymity, their comments are frank and fair. Their fairness is generally confirmed during the feedback process to the head and senior management of the school. Teachers generally acknowledge the validity and fairness of students' responses, though less consistently so when quizzed about students' work efforts. The qualities of good teachers identified by teachers show an often remarkable similarity to those mentioned by students.

Staff interview schedule on the learning culture

1. Do you think this school is a good school?
   Why? (Why not?)

2. There seems to be a dip in the school's popularity in Year 8.
   Do you have any views why?

3. XX% of all the students interviewed think they are good at your subject, and XX% think they are not good.
   Do you have any comments on these figures?

4. More than half the students interviewed quoted lack of understanding or lack of basic skills as reasons for not being good at particular subjects.
   Do you have any comments?

5. What are your views on the post-16 aspirations of students, and of their parents for them?

6. Nearly 70% of students interviewed estimated that they did an hour's homework or more every evening. Do you have any comments?

7. What are the elements of a good lesson?

8. What are the qualities of a good teacher?

Pupil orientation to learning

Introduction

Teachers' renewed interest in pedagogy has focused in particular on a number of aspects of teaching and learning – whether their own particular teaching repertoire is adequate to meet the range of learning styles of their students, whether their students are sufficiently equipped and skilled to take advantage of certain teaching and learning strategies, and whether the relevance of certain subjects in the curriculum is sufficiently justified to students.

Areas of enquiry in IQEA Project schools have included:

- the structure and organisation of lessons, and students' reactions to them;
- student views on what constitutes effective teaching;
- staff views on effective teaching;
- students' preferred learning styles;
- teaching strategies;
- students' attitudes towards various subjects.

Contents of section

Data collection sheet for lesson observations

Observations of teacher behaviour in classrooms

Schedule for observation of pupil classroom behaviour

Lesson reports based on observation schedule of pupil behaviour (1-pupil and 2-pupil versions)

Pupil questionnaire on classroom behaviour

Interview schedule on quality of learning and assessment (pupils)

Interview schedule on staff views on barriers to learning

Staff interview schedule on teaching and learning issues raised by pupils

Observation schedule of teaching strategies, based on Kolb's four learning styles

Pupil tick-list of preferred classroom activities

Interview schedule for pupils in Years 8, 9 and 10 on Technology

Data collection sheet for lesson observations

Purpose of instrument

- to record key events during a lesson.

Such events could include:

- instances of disruption by an individual student;
- a log of questions asked by a teacher;
- a log of how a lesson was structured in terms of teaching time, individual work etc.;
- a log of the participation of a particular student, or group of students, in a lesson.

Advice on administration

This observation schedule can be used by any adult, including a teacher known to the class. Students will have an initial curiosity about what the observer is doing, but are generally not phased by the presence of another adult in the room.

The ideal observation point is at the back of a room, the front being where the teacher is stationed. A corner table in a classroom organised in rows is best.

Some comments on findings

Whatever is being observed, teachers are very interested in sharing the findings. This may not be immediately possible, though some reassuring comment like, 'Thank you. I enjoyed that,' may be appropriate. Feedback to the class teacher involved should, however, be on the same day if possible. It may also be appropriate at times to feedback to any individual students being observed. A schedule appears later in the book for follow-up questioning of students after an observation.

Data collection sheet for lesson observations

Time	Detail of lesson

Observations of teacher behaviour in classrooms

(based upon a schedule in Flanders, N. (1965) *Teacher Influence, Pupil Attitudes, and Achievement*. Washington: US Office of Education)

Purpose of instrument

- to map the structure of a particular lesson in terms of teacher motivational behaviour (sections 1–3), teaching (sections 4–5), classroom organisation and discipline (6–7) and student involvement (8–10);

- to map lessons in terms of amounts of teacher talk (sections 1–7) and student talk (sections 8–9);

- to highlight particular features of a lesson (e.g. how often students' ideas are used by the teacher, how often questions are asked);

- to compare the structures of two lessons.

Advice on administration

The schedule is intended primarily for didactic lessons. The observation is quite demanding because it requires the observer to chart every utterance, of both teacher and students, that is relevant to the lesson. It is best used for a set period of the lesson, say half an hour.

The observation can be made by any adult, including a teacher known to the class. As it is mainly the teacher that is being observed, a good viewing station at the back of the classroom is vital.

The ticks recording each relevant utterance need to be counted, and the total for each section needs to be recorded as a percentage of the total number for the lesson observed. G/T refers to the grand total for each grouping of sections (see Purpose of instrument – above). Percentages for each of these groupings can also be calculated.

Some comments on findings

Lessons that go smoothly and are well planned tend to have small percentages recorded in sections 6 and 7. Teacher talk in most didactic lessons is at least double the amount of student talk. Teachers are often surprised by the number of questions they ask in a lesson.

Observations of teacher behaviour in classrooms

School:
Date:

Teacher behaviour	Lesson 1 details:				Lesson 2 details			
1. Accepts feelings								
2. Praises, encourages								
3. Uses pupil ideas								
SUBTOTALS	1.	2.	3.	G/T	1.	2.	3.	G/T
4. Asks questions								
5. Lectures								
SUBTOTALS	4.	5.		G/T	4.	5.		G/T
6. Gives directions								
7. Criticises, justifies authority								
SUBTOTALS	6.	7.		G/T	6.	7.		G/T
8. Pupil talk, response								
9. Pupil talk, initiate								
10. Silence, confusion								
SUBTOTALS	8.	9.	10.	G/T	8.	9.	10.	G/T

Schedule for observation of pupil classroom behaviour

(based upon a schedule in Good, T.L. and Brophy, J.E. (1978) *Looking in Classrooms*, 2nd edn. New York: Harper and Row)

Purpose of instrument

- to map the behaviour, and causes of the behaviour, of one or two students during a lesson;

- to calculate the amount of time spent by the student(s) on- and off-task;

- to gauge student reaction to different types of lesson organisation.

Advice on administration

A position at the back of the classroom, with the teacher at the front, is the best place for observation. As it is students who are being observed, it is more important to have a clear view of them than it is to have a clear view of the teacher. Any adult can do the observation, including a teacher known to the class.

Observations should be made every minute, on the minute. On-task behaviour is recorded as 1. It is best to have a clear knowledge of the observation schedule (see page 18) prior to the observation. If the students are unknown to the observer, an arrangement needs to be made with the teacher whereby the students are identified early on in the lesson. Registration is an ideal time for such identification.

For purposes of comparison of reactions to different teaching styles, students can be tracked throughout the school-day. The schedule can also be used to make notes on what the teacher is doing at any particular time. In this way a log of the lesson can be drawn up, matching teacher behaviour to student behaviour (see Lesson reports based on observation schedule of pupil behaviour – pages 19, 20).

Some comments on findings

Seventy-five per cent on-task behaviour is a reasonable performance for most students. Anything lower is a cause for concern, anything higher a cause for celebration. Teachers are often surprised by the high percentages of on-task behaviour of students perceived to be disruptive, and by the comparatively low percentages of some students deemed to be passive and hardworking.

Schedule for observation of pupil classroom behaviour

School: **Date:**   **Lesson:**

A. Pupil behaviour
1. Pays attention or actively works at assignment
2. Stares into space or closes eyes
3. Fidgets, taps, amuses self
4. Distracts others – entertains, jokes
5. Distracts others – questions, seeks help, investigates
6. Distracts others – attacks or teases
7. Leaves seat – goes to teacher
8. Leaves seat – wanders, runs, plays
9. Leaves seat – does approved action (what?)
10. Leaves seat – does forbidden action (what?)
11. Calls out answer
12. Calls out irrelevant comment (what?)
13. Calls out comment about teacher (what?)
14. Calls out comment about classmate (what?)
15. Deliberately causes disruption
16. Destroys property (whose? what?)
17. Leaves room without permission
18. Other (specify)

B. Apparent cause
What set off the behaviour?
1. No observable cause – suddenly began acting up
2. Appeared stumped by work, gave up
3. Finished work, had nothing to do
4. Distracted by classmate (who?)
5. Asked to respond or perform by teacher
6. Teacher checks or asks about progress on assigned work
7. Teacher calls for attention or return to work
8. Teacher praise (for what?)
9. Teacher criticism (for what?)
10. Teacher praises or rewards another student
11. Teacher criticises or punishes another student
12. Teacher refuses or delays permission request
13. Other (specify)

Notes:

Time		PUPIL 1 A	B	PUPIL 2 A	B
:	1.				
:	2.				
:	3.				
:	4.				
:	5.				
:	6.				
:	7.				
:	8.				
:	9.				
:	10.				
:	11.				
:	12.				
:	13.				
:	14.				
:	15.				
:	16.				
:	17.				
:	18.				
:	19.				
:	20.				
:	21.				
:	22.				
:	23.				
:	24.				
:	25.				
:	26.				
:	27.				
:	28.				
:	29.				
:	30.				
:	31.				
:	32.				
:	33.				
:	34.				
:	35.				
:	36.				
:	37.				
:	38.				
:	39.				
:	40.				

Lesson reports based on observation schedule of pupil behaviour

School: **Date:**

Time	Pupil behaviour	What is happening in lesson

Lesson reports based on observation schedule of pupil behaviour

Teacher: School: Date:

Time	Pupil 1	Pupil 2

Pupil questionnaire on classroom behaviour

Purpose of instrument

- to complement any data derived from observation of the student in the classroom;

- to match data derived from observation with student perceptions;

- to match teacher perceptions of the student with the student's self-perception;

- to clarify the reasons for observed behaviour(s).

Advice on administration

This schedule is best used after a period of tracking a particular student through a number of lessons. The student will need to be withdrawn about 20 minutes before the end of the last lesson to be observed. The interview should take place away from the classroom in a place where any disturbance is unlikely.

The student will be surprised that an observation has been taking place, but is unlikely to be offended if the purpose of the observation is explained in general terms, for example that staff are interested in the impact of certain teaching styles upon students' work efforts. Students are often quite flattered that they have been selected. In effect, teachers are generally interested in the impact of certain teaching styles upon disruptive students.

The schedule can be used as a questionnaire where a number of students have been tracked, and where separate interviews would be impractical. Clarification of certain behaviours observed in the course of lessons would, however, need to be done on a one-to-one basis.

Some comments on findings

Students' least preferred learning methods generally confirm impressions gained in the observation. Students' views of their own behaviour are generally realistic. Views of able students about their own ability are usually realistic, but those of less able students are more variable. Students who are perceived by their teachers as disruptive tend to underestimate their teachers' views of their ability.

Pupil questionnaire on classroom behaviour

Please tick answers as appropriate

1. **How do you prefer to learn?**

	Always	Often	Sometimes	Rarely
Group work				
Listening to teacher				
Quizzes and games				
Investigation work				
Experimental work				
Television and radio				
Role-play				
Solving problems				
Answering teacher questions				
Individual work				
Drawing				
Demonstrations				
Using computers				
Copying notes				

2. **How would you describe your behaviour in lessons?**

Always well behaved ☐
Usually well behaved ☐
Sometimes badly behaved ☐
Often badly behaved ☐

3. **Pupils who work hard in lessons are made fun of**

Always ☐
Often ☐
Sometimes ☐
Rarely ☐
Never ☐

4. **How would you describe your ability?**

Very able ☐
Higher than average ☐
Average ☐
Lower than average ☐

5. I get praised during lessons

Always ☐
Often ☐
Sometimes ☐
Rarely ☐
Never ☐

6. How do you think your teachers would describe your behaviour in lessons?

Always well behaved ☐
Usually well behaved ☐
Sometimes badly behaved ☐
Often badly behaved ☐

7. Do you work better when the teacher tells you where to sit or when you sit with friends?

8. How do you think teachers would describe your ability?

Very able ☐
Higher than average ☐
Average ☐
Lower than average ☐

9. Do you think teachers pay enough attention to you?

10. Do you bring the right equipment to lessons?

Always ☐
Often ☐
Sometimes ☐
Rarely ☐
Never ☐

11. Do you enjoy coming to school?

Interview schedule on quality of learning and assessment (pupils)

Purpose of instrument

- to determine students' views on what constitutes a good lesson;
- to determine students' views on what constitutes a good teacher.

Advice on administration

This schedule is best suited to secondary students. It is best administered by someone who doesn't teach the student, or group of students, being interviewed. Interviews can be with single students or groups of up to three students from the same class. The interviews need to take place in a space away from the bustle of school business. Depending on the size of the group, interviews can take between 20 and 30 minutes.

Some comments on findings

Students of all ages tend to dislike the lecture as a teaching strategy. Worksheets are also disliked. This may be because they remain the most common form of teaching strategy used in secondary schools. Students tend to like an element of activity or practical work in a lesson. They generally favour group work, insisting (sometimes vehemently) that they discuss work in such a situation. They do not mind writing if it is not for the whole lesson. They favour well-structured lessons with clear rules of conduct laid down by the teacher or negotiated with them.

Teachers tend to be judged by all age groups in terms of their personality, and only secondarily for their teaching ability. Qualities valued include a sense of humour, approachability, a willingness to give individual help, and empathy. Strictness is not liked, but firmness is accepted when it comes hand in hand with fairness. This sense of justice and fairness is particularly emphasised by Year 9 and Year 10 students.

Interview schedule on quality of learning and assessment (pupils)

1. Do you like school?

2. What do you like most about school?

3. What makes a good lesson?

4. What does a teacher do at the beginning of a lesson?

5. How is the class organised in a good lesson?

6. What sort of work does the class do in a good lesson?

7. What does the teacher do at the end of a good lesson?

8. Do you behave differently in a good lesson?

9. What makes a good teacher?

Interview schedule on staff views on barriers to learning

Purpose of instrument

- to determine staff's views on students' orientations to work;
- to assess opportunities provided for independent learning;
- to determine staff's views on what constitutes a good lesson.

Advice on administration

Given the sensitivity of Question 8, the interview is best done with individual members of staff, in a place where there is little chance of interruption. It is also best administered by someone who is not a teaching member of the school staff.

The schedule can also be used as a questionnaire.

Some comments on findings

Teachers generally underestimate the aspirations of their students, particularly the numbers who wish to enter Further or Higher Education. Views on the amounts of homework which students claim to do are variable.

Teachers stress the organisational and administrative elements of a good lesson, rather than the part played by the impact of their personalities upon the class.

Where teachers feel secure about the anonymising of their comments, they can be very forthright in their views of the changes necessary in the management of the school to improve the quality of teaching and learning. Disciplinary issues often feature prominently in their comments.

Interview schedule on staff views on barriers to learning

1. What are your views on students' academic aspirations?

2. How do you feel about their parents' aspirations for them?

3. Most pupils claim to do (xxx, according to interview findings) hours' homework most nights.
   Have you any comments on this?

4. How would you define a pupil working hard in a lesson?
   Do most of your pupils work hard in your lessons?

5. How do you assess whether a pupil is learning?

6. Do you allow pupils to organise part of their own learning?
   In what way?

7. How would you describe a good lesson?

8. Is there anything that the school could do to improve the quality of classroom teaching and learning in this school?

Staff interview schedule on teaching and learning issues raised by pupils

Purpose of instrument

- to test students' views on various aspects of teaching and learning with staff.

Advice on administration

This is a useful form of schedule to administer after a review has been made of students' views on teaching and learning in the school. It enables staff to articulate, defend or comment upon teaching practices within the school. Such a schedule is best administered to individual members of staff in a quiet area in the school. Anonymity of comments must be assured, and for this reason the interview is best administered by a trusted colleague or by a complete outsider, perhaps an Adviser who has no regular contact with the school.

Interviews should take about 20 minutes.

Some comments on findings

Teachers generally acknowledge the fairness of students' comments, and rarely reject them out of hand as ill-founded.

Staff interview schedule on teaching and learning issues raised by pupils

1. The pupil interviews suggested that most pupils had warm feelings towards the school. However, there seems to be a 'culture shock' in Y10, where pupils become aware of the 'seriousness of learning'.
   Do you have any comments on this?

2. There was some student comment about work being repeated, particularly in Y7. There was also some comment about the relevance and worth of some work.
   Are these issues for you?

3. There seems to be a general lack, and indeed a cynicism typified by attitudes to Records of Achievement, of student reflection on their learning, except in the Sixth Form.
   There seems to be little or no private research except at the two ends of the school.
   Do you have any comments?

4. Students' views vary on the effectiveness of group work, and how it should be organised.
   What are your views on group work, and how do you organise it?

5. Marking and teacher comments were valued by students as indicators of how they were progressing, but there seemed to be a lack of specific advice in marking on how students could improve.
   Do you have any comments on this?

Observation schedule of teaching strategies, based on Kolb's four learning styles

Purpose of instrument

- to map and categorise the different teaching strategies used in a lesson, or in a series of lessons.

Advice on administration

The theoretical underpinning of this technique is briefly explained in the diagram on the next page. Teachers who are interested in further detail should consult the following references:

Hopson, B. and Scally, M. (1982) *Lifeskills Teaching Programmes No. 2*. Leeds: Lifeskills Associates.
Kolb, D. A. (1984) *Experiential Learning: Experience as the Source of Learning and Development*. Englewood Cliffs, New Jersey: Prentice-Hall.

The schedule lists 38 teaching strategies, and categorises them according to Kolb's typology. For ease of use, the strategies are listed alphabetically. The observer should have a sound knowledge of the structure of the schedule prior to the first observation. Lessons should be observed from a part of the classroom providing a clear view of the teacher. The observation can be undertaken by any adult.

The incidence of a particular strategy during a lesson should be indicated with a tick. Because the point of the exercise is to map the range of strategies employed by a teacher, it is unnecessary to put more than one tick against each strategy. At the end of the lesson the number of ticks for each category should be recorded in the boxes provided at the bottom of each sheet.

Different lessons within the same department can be mapped to provide a profile of the teaching strategies employed. Different lessons in all departments can be mapped to give a school-wide profile. Where a number of lessons have been observed it is best to convert categories of teaching strategies into percentages.

Some comments on findings

Kolb argues that unless teachers cater for all four kinds of learning style, certain groups of students will miss out educationally. In secondary schools the predominant teaching strategies observed favour convergers and assimilators (see diagram). In subjects like Science and Technology, which are dependent to a great extent upon experimentation, demonstration and practice of skills, this is hardly surprising. But the profile is often little different in other subjects less dependent upon such teaching strategies.

It is clear from the categories that the teaching and learning activities favoured by accommodators and divergers involve a high level of social interaction independent of the teacher. Converger and assimilator activities are more easily controlled by the teacher.

Kolb's four learning styles

SENSING/ FEELING
Concrete experiences

Accommodators
(enthusiastic)

Divergers
(imaginative)

DOING
Testing implications
of concepts in new
situations

WATCHING
Observation and
reflections

Convergers
(practical)

Assimilators
(logical)

THINKING
Formation of abstract concepts and generalisations

Observation schedule of teaching strategies, based on Kolb's four learning styles

Date: **Lesson:**

Teaching strategies   **Incidence**

Accuracy stressed	C	
Accurate recall	As	
Action planning	As	
Brainstorming	D	
Case-study	As	
Choice of activities	C	
Classwork	As	
Clear goals expressed	C	
Comprehension	C	
Data collection	As	
Demonstrations	As	
Discussion	D	
Group interaction	D	
Group work organised	Ac	
Gut feelings asked for	Ac	
Hand outs	As	
Investigations	D	
Lecture	As	
Mistakes allowed	Ac	
Note taking	C	
Open-ended questions asked	D	
Paired work	D	
Planning of work by pupils	C	
Practising skills	C	
Problem-solving	C	
Reflection on experience	D	
Relevance of work explained	C	
Reporting back methods varied	Ac	
Role-play	D	
Scientific experiments	C	
Simulations used	Ac	
Specialisms tapped	As	
Testing	C	
Thoroughness stressed	C	
Variety of approaches	Ac	
Video	As	
Working alone	C, As	
Worksheets	C	

Ac		D		
C		As		

Pupil tick-list of preferred classroom activities

Purpose of instrument

- to determine students' preferred classroom activities.

Advice on administration

This schedule can be administered as part of a classroom lesson, with each student filling in their own tick-list. Some of the activities may need some amplification by the teacher.

The list can also be used for students to record which activities they meet in school lessons; additionally, it can be used by departments, as is the case with the specimen schedule.

The list coincides with the previous observation schedule. Teachers need to fill in the appropriate category of learning style once the tick-list has been completed. It is then possible, by collating all the responses of a particular teaching group and converting each category into a percentage, to draw up a profile of preferred learning styles. This can be compared with the teaching strategies profile derived from lesson observations (see previous instrument).

Some comments on findings

Students generally favour more accommodator and diverger activities than they usually get. Most of the classroom activities that get little enthusiastic support in students' tick-lists are converger and assimilator activities. Most students show fairly catholic tastes in classroom activities, invariably ticking more than half the activities in the list.

Pupil tick-list of preferred classroom activities

Please tick which of these classroom activities you prefer in Maths lessons.
Add any comments you wish to.

Type of activity		Comments
One in which accuracy is important		
One where I have to recall accurately		
One where I am involved in the planning of work		
Brainstorming		
One where we look at examples		
Choice of activities		
Classwork		
One where clear goals are expressed by the teacher		
Comprehension		
Data collection		
Demonstrations		
Discussion		
One where we are allowed to talk in groups		
One where the teacher organises groupwork		
Gut feelings asked for		
Hand outs are given out		
Investigations		
Lecture		
One where I'm allowed to make mistakes		
Note taking		
One where lots of answers are possible		
Paired work		
One where I plan the work		
Practising skills		
Problem-solving		
One where I'm asked to think about my experiences		
One where the reason I'm doing it is clear		
One where we can report back in different ways		
Role-play		
One that involves experiments		
One that involves real life situations		
One that uses my particular skill		
Testing		
One that needs me to be thorough		
One where the teacher uses different teaching methods		
Video		
Working alone		
One where worksheets are given out		

I am in Year _____

I am male/female
(circle the right one)

Interview schedule for pupils in Years 8, 9 and 10 on Technology

Purpose of instrument

- to determine students' attitudes towards Technology as a school subject;
- to assess students' self-esteem in the subject;
- to determine how students arrive at their self-assessment.

Advice on administration

The interview lasts only ten minutes, so a large number of students can be interviewed in a comparatively short time. Because students are being asked to comment upon their own work performances, it is best that they are interviewed individually. Because they are so short, the interviews can be conducted in a place near to where the lesson is taking place. This avoids serious disruption of the lesson, particularly if it is a practical session.

The schedule can obviously be used for different subjects. It is best administered by someone who does not teach the subject to the students being interviewed.

Some comments on findings

Students are frank when the anonymity of their responses is guaranteed. They tend to take questions about their ability and their enjoyment of a particular subject seriously. Most students look to teacher comments or test marks on which to base the assessments of their ability.

Students in Years 9 and 10 tend to be fairly utilitarian in their views about the value of certain subjects, views that are quite crucial in their choice of option subjects in Year 9 and GCSE subjects in Year 10. Interviews in Year 8 give an early indicator to possible option choices in Year 9, and alert certain departments to justify and 'sell' their subjects more energetically to students.

Interview schedule for pupils in Years 8, 9 and 10 on Technology

Year   8   9   10   Boy   Girl

1. Do you think Technology is an important school subject? Yes/No
    Why/why not?

2. Are you good at Technology? Yes/No
    How do you know?

3. Do you enjoy Technology? Yes/No
    Why/why not?

4. What would you like to do in Technology?

Independent learning

Introduction

Enabling students to learn independently is a key objective of most schools. Most primary and secondary schools now set homework. Coursework is an important element of many GCSE courses. Many school subjects lend themselves to an investigational approach to learning.

Many of the IQEA Project schools with which we have worked have chosen as their focus for improvement the development of independent learning in their schools. Areas of enquiry have included:

- the extent to which the conditions for independent learning already exist within the school;
- problem-solving and research opportunities available within the curriculum;
- student reflection and self-assessment;
- student evaluation of initiatives to encourage independent learning;
- the effectiveness of schools' homework policies.

Contents of section

Pupil interview schedule on the learning culture of the school

Interview schedules for pupils on collaborative learning

Pupil interview schedule on effective groupwork

Pupil questionnaire on library use

Staff questionnaire on library use

Pupil interview schedule on Early Morning Work at a primary school

Pupil interview schedule on target-setting

Staff's homework survey

Pupils' homework survey

Parents' homework survey

Parents' questionnaire on homework

Interview schedule on use of Homework Club (non-users)
(occasional users)
(regular users)

Pupil interview schedule on the learning culture of the school

Purpose of instrument

- to determine students' views on the extent to which the conditions for effective independent learning already exist within a school.

Advice on administration

Single-gender groups of three students in the same teaching group are best for this interview. The interview is quite a long one, lasting up to 30 minutes, so it should be administered in a quiet area where disturbances are unlikely.

Some comments on findings

Section A is intended as a warm-up section. Negative comments about some lessons and some teachers are likely from Year 9 and Year 10 students, who will also tend to identify social relationships as the best part of school. Students at the start or end of their secondary school careers will show some enthusiasm for the school's facilities, and for some teachers.

Most schools provide opportunities for research and problem-solving, and students are generally aware of where resources and equipment can be found. There may be some abuse of students who ask questions in class. Students are adamant that comments are intended to be light-hearted, but some students, particularly girls, admit that it has a dampening effect upon them.

Students tend to enjoy groupwork, and claim to do a lot of work in groups. They tend to be extremely dependent upon teacher comments and grades in tests in arriving at self-assessments of their work. Students seem to reflect only rarely upon their work, are generally reluctant to seek help on ways they could improve their learning, and receive very little specific written advice from teachers on this aspect of their work. This may in part explain the fairly dismissive attitude towards the value of filling in Records of Achievement beyond Year 8.

© IQEA – *Collecting Information for School Improvement*

Pupil interview schedule on the learning culture of the school

Section A: Attitudes to school

1 (a) What do you like most about school?

(b) What do you like least about the school?

Section B: Independent learning

2 (a) Do you know where to find things like equipment and books?

(b) Do you ever look for information on your own initiative?
For which subjects?

(c) Where do you look?

(d) Do you do problem solving in lessons?
Which ones?
What sort of problems do you get given?

(e) Do you ask questions in lessons?
Do your classmates ever make fun of you for asking questions?

(f) Do you ever think about what you have done in a particular lesson?

Section C: Groupwork

3 (a) Do you ever work with other students?
In which lessons?

(b) Do you usually get a lot done when working in this way?

Section D: Self-assessment

4 (a) How do you check what you have learnt from activities in school?

(b) Do you ever talk to anyone about how you could learn more or about what you could
improve on?

(c) Are you involved in reporting your own progress?

Interview schedules for pupils on collaborative learning

Purpose of instrument

- to evaluate a pilot project in collaborative learning in a primary school;
- to assess whether students need further guidance in working effectively in groups.

Advice on administration

Year 2 students talk naturally to adults in a classroom setting, so where the working buzz is not too loud it may be possible to conduct the interview inside or just outside the classroom. Infants in particular may be vociferous and unrestrained in their comments, so the interviewer may find it difficult to cope with more than two students at a time. Junior students may be more restrained, so any size of group up to four is possible, as long as each student gets a turn to answer. Primary school children are usually less critical of their teachers than secondary students, so interviews could be undertaken by the class teacher without compromising the authenticity of most students' comments.

Some comments on findings

Although most Infants are used to working cooperatively in a range of activities, they are less used to working collaboratively to produce an end-product. They seem to enjoy such activities, however, are tolerant of any shortcomings in their partner and are prepared to help them.

Junior students also enjoy collaborative activities, but are more likely than Infants to allow personal animosities to affect their work. They find it more difficult to work effectively with students they say they do not like, and such individual rivalries can disrupt the working of a group.

Interview schedules for pupils on collaborative learning

Year 2

Do you remember when you worked together?

What happened? (appropriate prompt questions)

Did you argue?

What about?

Did you help each other?

How?

Were you happy with what you did/wrote/painted . . . ?

Do you like working with friends?

Why?

Do you like it more than working by yourself?

Why?

Year 6

Do you prefer working by yourself, or working in a group?

Why?

Was (named activity) better done in a group, or would you have preferred to do it by yourself?

Why?

Are there any disadvantages to groupwork?

Do you ever argue?

When?

How do you settle arguments?

Do they ever spill over to outside the classroom?

Are you happy with what the group produces?

How do you all decide you are happy?

Is what the group produces better than what you could do by yourself?

Pupil interview schedule on effective groupwork

Purpose of instrument

- to assess the incidence of groupwork in the school;
- to discover students' views on the best way to select groups;
- to discover students' views on effective groupwork practice.

Advice on administration

In order to instigate a good debate on the value or otherwise of single-sex groups, it is best to administer this schedule to a group of two girls and two boys. The interview will take a minimum of 20 minutes, and needs to take place away from the classroom. It is best administered by an adult who does not teach the group. The schedule can also be used as a questionnaire, although the debate about single-sex groupings may not provide such rich data.

Some comments on findings

Students enjoy groupwork, and generally claim to work hard in groups. Most schools provide some opportunities for groupwork in a variety of subjects, although groupwork in Maths and Art seems rare. Few schools seem to provide coaching or instruction in how to work effectively in groups.

Students in secondary schools tend to prefer to work in friendship groups, which are usually single-sex groupings. They are more tolerant of groupings imposed by teachers after Year 9, when they start distinguishing between friends and students with whom they are prepared to work. Students are appreciative of the expertise of individual students at all ages, but particularly in the examination years of Years 10 and 11.

Pupil interview schedule on effective groupwork

Groupwork is work undertaken by three or more pupils on a shared task.

1. How often do you do groupwork?
   In which subjects?

2. Who chooses the groups?

3. Which method of deciding groups do you prefer?
   Why?

4. Do you like groupwork?
   Why?

5. How do you feel about varying the group memberships?

6. Describe a situation where groupwork works really well.

7. Describe one where it doesn't.

Pupil questionnaire on library use

Purpose of instrument

- to determine the amount of staff direction to students to use the library;
- to determine how, and how often, students use the library;
- to determine students' views on how the library could be improved;
- to assess the amount of student use of the library during the school day.

Advice on administration

This particular questionnaire was issued to every student who entered the school's library during school-time, and over lunch-time. This required the person distributing the questionnaires to be near the entrance both to distribute and collect questionnaires. A tray was also provided at the library desk where students could leave completed questionnaires.

Where the library is used by the community as well, a librarian could be used to distribute questionnaires, although not every student goes to the reception desk.

Some comments on findings

Some lessons, including study periods for Years 12 and 13 students, were timetabled in the library. While some teachers do direct students to specific library resources, many students work in the school library without consulting any of these resources, relying on textbooks as their main source. Homework is a popular library activity.

Suggestions for improving the library tend to concentrate on relaxing any restrictions on its accessibility to students, on increasing the numbers of specific types of resources and on improving catering facilities.

© IQEA – *Collecting Information for School Improvement*

Pupil questionnaire on library use

Please answer for yesterday's and today's lessons.

Date: **Class:**   **Girl/Boy**

1. Did you have any lessons yesterday/today where you were asked to use the library?
                              YES/NO

2. In which lessons were you asked?

3. What have you been asked to do in the library?

4. Is this the reason for your visit?   YES/NO
   If NO, what is the reason for your visit?

5. What else do you use the library for?

6. Do you have a library card?   YES/NO

7. What books do you have out at the moment?

8. How often do you borrow:
   - (a) books?
   - (b) videos?
   - (c) CDs?

9. Have you any comments on the library, for example how it could be made better?

Thank you for taking the time to answer this questionnaire.

Staff questionnaire on library use

Purpose of instrument

- to provide a snapshot of the extent to which staff direct students to use the library;
- to determine what part library use plays in the delivery of the school curriculum.

Advice on administration

This can be undertaken as a department-wide or school-wide exercise. The questionnaire should be given on the same day to all members of the department or staff. It takes about ten minutes to complete, so could be distributed at the beginning of a staff meeting.

The data can be used in conjunction with that derived from the pupil questionnaire (see previous instrument).

Some comments on findings

Teachers are likely to direct students to use library resources, and students claim to use their own books and their local libraries as well as their school library. Very few secondary schools seem to coach students in the effective use of libraries, perhaps assuming that primary schools have provided such instruction.

The increasing number of students with access to the Internet suggests that coaching in its use needs to be addressed by schools.

Staff questionnaire on library use

Please answer for yesterday's lessons.

Date: Department:

1. Did you request or encourage any pupils to use the library? YES/NO

2. Could you specify below the classes involved, and what uses you recommended?

3. Have you any comments on the library's provision and accessibility for pupils?

4. Is library use built into the schemes of work of your department? YES/NO

5. Which library skills do you teach in your department?

6. How often do you use the library
   (a) for your own work?
   (b) with a class?

Thank you for taking the time to fill in this questionnaire.

Pupil interview schedule on Early Morning Work at a primary school

Purpose of instrument

- to evaluate a pilot project on independent learning;
- to seek students' views on the rationale underpinning the initiative.

Advice on administration

The schedule can be administered to mixed-gender groups of four students. It can be administered in a school corridor, though a quiet room should be used if one is available. The interviewer can be a class teacher, though ideally not the one who teaches the group.

Some comments on findings

A number of students will be unaware that any change in practice has taken place. Some students in this particular instance were critical of the length of time spent on independent learning activities first thing in the morning, and also the quality of some of the learning activities provided by teachers. A few identified the teachers' rationale for introducing Early Morning Work – that there was a problem of lesson disruption in the school caused by the late arrival of many children.

Pupil interview schedule on Early Morning Work at a primary school

1. What do you do when you come into the classroom every morning?

2. Why do you think you are asked to do that?

3. Do you like doing that?

4. Why/why not?

5. How could it be made better?

Pupil interview schedule on target-setting

Purpose of instrument

- to evaluate a pilot project on target-setting;
- to assess how widespread is the practice of target-setting in the school.

Advice on administration

The interview can be administered to single-gender or mixed-gender groups of three or four students in the same year, and is suitable for the whole secondary range. The schedule can be administered by a teacher not known to the group, or another adult. It is best undertaken in a quiet area away from the classroom. Interviews take about 20 minutes, so about 18 groups can be interviewed in the course of a normal school-day.

Some comments on findings

There is often some inconsistency in the implementation of school-wide initiatives, with practice falling off after Years 7 and 8. There may often be little evidence of teacher-student negotiation of targets. Working practices requiring a degree of bureaucracy, for example the filling in of individual student work planners, often fall into disuse in Years 9 and 10, due in part to teacher reaction to student apathy.

Sixth formers often see the value of such practices retrospectively, and are largely an untapped source of propaganda for justifying initiatives like target-setting to younger students.

Pupil interview schedule on target-setting

1. Are targets explained clearly to you at the start of each lesson?

2. Do you know what you have to do to achieve these targets?

3. Are you involved in setting your own targets?

4. How do you know when you've achieved a target?

5. Are targets always achievable?

6. How do you record the achievement of a target?

7. Are long-term targets set?

Staff's homework survey
Pupils' homework survey
Parents' homework survey

Purpose of instruments

- to match staff, student and parent expectations about homework.

Advice on administration

Questionnaires can be given to all students in a school, or those in a particular year-group. All staff should be given one, and also the parents of all students of the particular sample chosen. The students' and parents' questionnaires take about five minutes to complete, longer if comments are added. The staff's questionnaire could take up to 15 minutes.

Some comments on findings

Students claim to do less homework than staff claim to set, and less than parents hope they do. Girls get slightly more help from their parents than boys – both suggest that their parents help less than they say.

Girls like doing homework with music on, boys with the television on. Staff favour a quiet working atmosphere. Students are more confident than their parents about the adequacy of home-based resources for doing homework. Staff are more enthusiastic about establishing Homework Clubs than students and their parents.

The return rate for parental questionnaires will be low.

Staff's homework survey

Department:

1. I set the following amounts of homework every week:

Year 7	Year 8	Year 9	Year 10	Year 11

2. I regard the main purpose of homework as ...

Do you ever justify homework to students?

3. I would estimate the percentage of parents signing planners to be as follows:

Every night	
Most nights	
Occasionally	
Rarely	
Never	

4.   Describe the working environment you would hope that most homes provide for students to do their homework.

5.   What are your views on having a Homework Club at school?
     Would you be prepared to support it with your time?

Thank you for your time and patience in filling in this survey sheet.

Pupils' homework survey

Please tick the boxes which best fit your views.
Please feel free to add any comments beside any of the questions.

I am in Year _____ I am a Girl/Boy (circle the right one)

1.   Every evening I expect to do   **Comments**

no homework	
at least half an hour's homework	
at least an hour's homework	
at least an hour and a half's homework	
at least two hours' homework	
at least two and a half hours' homework	
at least three hours' homework	
more	

2.   My parents discuss my homework with me

every night	
most nights	
occasionally	
rarely	
never	

3.   My parents sign my planner

every night	
most nights	
occasionally	
rarely	
never	

4.   I do my homework

in my own room	
in a room with the family around	
with music on	
in front of the television	
at a friend's house	
somewhere else (where?)	

(tick more than one box if necessary)

5.   At home

I have the books and equipment necessary to do my homework	
I don't always have them	
I would prefer to do homework in a Homework Club at the school after school	

6.   Parents' help

My parents help me with my homework	
My parents would like to help me with my homework	
My mates help me with my homework	
Homework is best done on my own	
I can't see the point of much of the homework I get	

Thank you for your time and patience in filling in this survey sheet.

Parents' homework survey

If you have more than one child at the school, we would be grateful if you could fill in one of these survey sheets for each of them.
Please tick the boxes which best fit your views.
Please feel free to add any comments beside any of the questions.

My child is in Year

1. Every evening I expect my child to do   **Comments**

no homework	
at least half an hour's homework	
at least an hour's homework	
at least an hour and a half's homework	
at least two hours' homework	
at least two and a half hours' homework	
at least three hours' homework	
more	

2. I discuss homework set for my child

every night	
most nights	
occasionally	
rarely	
never	

3. I make comments in my child's planner

every night	
most nights	
occasionally	
rarely	
never	

4. My child does his/her homework   **Comments**

in their own room	
in a room with the family around	
with music on	
in front of the television	
at a friend's house	
somewhere else (where?)	

(tick more than one box if necessary)

5. At home

we do have the books and equipment in the house necessary for my child to do their homework	
we don't always have them	
we would prefer homework to be done in a Homework Club at the school after school	

6. Helping our child

We help our child with their homework	
We would like to help our child with their homework	
Homework is best done by our child without our help	
Our child doesn't ask for help with their homework	
We can't see the point of much of the homework set	

Thank you for your time and patience in filling in this survey sheet.

Parents' questionnaire on homework

Purpose of instrument

- to find out parents' views on the rationale underpinning homework;

- to determine how parents evaluate homework.

Advice on administration

Return rates for parental questionnaires are poor, so it may be useful to distribute them at parents' evenings, providing an area where they can be filled in. This particular questionnaire should take about ten minutes to complete, though some parents will want to write at length on some questions.

Some comments on findings

Parents approve of homework being set. Most look to homework improving study skills, but are concerned that it is not set regularly enough. Homework enables parents to find out what their children are doing at school, and also to help them with the work set.

Parents questionnaire on homework

1. Do you approve of homework being set?

2. If yes, what do you think is the purpose of homework?
    (tick as appropriate)

    - raising standards
    - allowing more work to be done
    - allowing more effective use of school-time
    - improving study skills
    - improving attitudes to learning
    - others (please state)

3. Does the homework your child is set achieve these purposes?
    If not, why not?

4. How much homework does your child do in an average evening?

    - varies
    - half an hour
    - one hour
    - one and a half hours
    - two hours
    - more
    - don't know

5. Have you any suggestions about making homework more useful to your child?

6. Does homework help you

    - find out what your child is doing at school?
    - find out how well your child is doing?
    - help your child?
    - in other ways? (please state)

Thank you for filling in this questionnaire.

Interview schedule on use of Homework Club: (non-users)
(occasional users)
(regular users)

Purpose of instruments

- to determine the factors causing students to use, or not to use, a Homework Club;
- to determine students' views on how to improve the Homework Club.

Advice on administration

Because the schedule focuses on individual working habits, it is best administered to individual students by an adult not involved in teaching in the school. Interviews take only about ten minutes, so for minimum disruption of lessons they can be administered in a corridor or quiet space near to the student's classroom.

Some comments on findings

Key factors quoted by regular users of the club were access to computers and access to adults as resources. Non-users also rated these factors as important, but had access to both at home. The timing of the club – after school – was also important for some non-users who had distances to travel home. They indicated that they would attend a lunch-time Homework Club. Most non-users, however, expressed a preference for working at home.

Interview schedule on use of Homework Club: non-users

1. Why do you choose not to use the Homework Club?

2. What resources do you have at home?

3. What do you think of Homework Club?

4. Would you make any changes to Homework Club that would make you want to go to it?

Interview schedule on use of Homework Club: occasional users

1. Why did you choose to use the Homework Club?

2. What kind of homework did you do in Homework Club?

3. What are the main subjects you did in Homework Club?

4. Which resources did you use?

5. Why did you choose to stop going?

6. What do your parents think of Homework Club?

7. Would you make any changes to Homework Club?

Interview schedule on use of Homework Club: regular users

1. Why do you use the Homework Club?

2. What kind of homework do you do in Homework Club?

3. What are the main subjects you do in Homework Club?

4. Which resources do you use?

5. Are you doing *more* homework than you used to before Homework Club?

6. Are you doing *better quality* homework than before Homework Club?
   How do you know?

7. What do your parents think of Homework Club?

8. Have they commented on your work since you started Homework Club?

9. Have your teachers made any comments?

10. Would you make any changes to Homework Club?

Teacher–pupil relations

Introduction

Good teacher-student relationships are a vital feature of effective teaching and learning. Our research in IQEA schools suggests that, where teachers are able to provide a safe and caring working environment for students, effective learning takes place. Students in such an environment have high levels of self-esteem, and are motivated. They readily identify the qualities of teachers for whom they work – among others, a sense of humour, a willingness to give individual help, firmness tempered with fairness, and a concern for them as individuals.

Where teacher-student relationships are poor, there can be a number of consequences. Students may underachieve or, in extreme cases, truant; classes may be disrupted, and various disciplinary measures may result in students missing part of their education.

Teacher behaviours to develop student self-esteem and motivation may be an integral part of most teachers' repertoires, but they can also be learnt. Some of the instruments in this section identify such behaviours.

Contents of section

Questionnaire on pupil self-esteem in academic work

Interview schedule for pupils on self-esteem

Interview schedule on teaching and learning issues for disenchanted Y10 pupils

Interview schedule on motivation of streamed pupils in the middle band

Observation schedule on pupil motivation and teacher behaviour

Questionnaire on pupil motivation and teacher behaviour

Interview schedule for pupil views on classroom order

Questionnaire on pupil self-esteem in academic work

Purpose of instrument

- to determine and compare levels of students' self-esteem in various school subjects;

- to determine and compare students' career aspirations, and their views on their parents' aspirations for them;

- to determine and compare levels of student commitment to independent learning;

- to determine and compare students' views on the qualities of effective lessons and effective teachers.

Advice on administration

These questionnaires can be given to individual year-groups or to a whole school. They can be given to different sub-groupings within the school – this particular questionnaire was coded *d/man* in the corner of the second page, and was given to students who were deemed by staff to be demotivated. Another set, coded *m/man*, were distributed to motivated students. They are designed to be done in school during a tutorial or registration period, and take about 15 minutes to complete.

Some comments on findings

Unsurprisingly, motivated students tend to like school more than demotivated ones. School as a place for meeting friends is more important for motivated students, who also show higher levels of self-esteem in all subjects except those with a strong practical element, like PE, Art and Drama. Both groups of students tend to have very firm views on their ability in Maths, Science and English, compared to other subjects.

Motivated students are more prepared to highlight personal shortcomings as a contributory cause of their difficulties in various subjects. They are slightly keener to undertake further study after school, though there is little difference in the career aspirations of each group. Motivated students do more homework than demotivated ones, although the gap narrows during the GCSE years. Both groups are equally inclined to turn to teachers and family members for help, but motivated students in Years 9 and 10 are more likely to seek help from their friends than demotivated ones.

Both groups identify enjoyment as an important element of a good lesson. Enjoyment stems from the personality and professional expertise of the teacher. Teachers need to have a sense of fun, and to be approachable. They need to be firm without being strict or disrespectful to students. Students from Years 9 and 10 in both groups value qualities which enable a personal approach to a teacher for help to be made.

Questionnaire on pupil self-esteem in academic work

Please answer these questions as fully as you can.
I am in tutor group:

1. **Do you like school?**   YES ☐   NO ☐
    (Please tick)

    Please give reasons for your answer:

2. **Which subjects are you good at?** (Please tick)

English ☐	Music ☐	Technology ☐
Maths ☐	Art ☐	PE/Games ☐
Science ☐	Drama ☐	PSE ☐
French ☐	History ☐	Youth Award ☐
German ☐	Geography ☐	
Urdu ☐	RS ☐	
Sociology ☐	IT ☐	

    Any others? (Please say which ones)

3. **Are there any subjects you're not good at?** (Please tick)

English ☐	Music ☐	Technology ☐
Maths ☐	Art ☐	PE/Games ☐
Science ☐	Drama ☐	PSE ☐
French ☐	History ☐	Youth Award ☐
German ☐	Geography ☐	
Urdu ☐	RS ☐	
Sociology ☐	IT ☐	

    Any others? (Please say which ones)

    Why aren't you good at them?

4. **What do you want to do after you leave school?**

5. **What would your parents like you to do?**

6. **How much homework do you do every night?** (Please tick)

None	☐
About half an hour	☐
About an hour	☐
About two hours	☐
More	☐
Other (Please say how much)	☐

7. **If you need help with any of your work, who do you go to?** (Please tick)

Teacher	☐
Parent	☐
Friend	☐
Other (Please say who)	☐

8. **Think of a good lesson you've had recently. Why was it good?**

9. **Without naming him/her, tell me about your favourite teacher.**
   What is special about him/her?

Thank you for giving up your time to fill in this questionnaire.

© IQEA – *Collecting Information for School Improvement*

Interview schedule for pupils on self-esteem

Purpose of instrument

- to determine and compare levels of student orientation to school;
- to determine factors contributing to students' views about school.

Advice on administration

While this schedule was administered as a follow-up to the previous questionnaire in this section, it can stand on its own. It takes about 20 minutes to administer.

As with the questionnaire, students can be identified as motivated or demotivated, according to staff perceptions. Interviews are ideally conducted with individual students, but it is possible to administer to groups of three, preferably single-sex groupings. Some copy-cat answering may, however, result. The interviews should be administered in a quiet area by an adult who is not a teacher at the school.

Some comments on findings

Motivated students will rate their school more highly than demotivated ones, and will have more knowledge of other schools. The perceived quality of student-teacher relationships and of lessons are important factors in the assessments of both groups of a good school.

Motivated students are happier at school than demotivated ones except in Year 10, where levels of happiness are more equal. They are more likely to have most of their friends in school, and are more likely than demotivated students to live within walking distance of the school. Motivated students are more likely to spend breaktimes talking to friends, and are more likely to attend break-time clubs and activities.

Motivated students look more to teacher grades than demotivated ones in order to justify views of their ability. Both groups stress the importance of enjoyment and having a good relationship with the teacher as factors in being good at a particular subject.

More motivated students want to go to university and know people who have been to university. Their reasons for wanting to go to university are more materialistic than those of demotivated students.

Interview schedule for pupils on self-esteem

1. Is this a good school?
   How do you know?

2. Are you happy at this school?
   Are you more or less happy than you were in your primary school?
   than you were in Year 7?
   or are you about the same?
   (What has made the difference?)

3. Are most of your friends school friends?
   Do you walk to school or catch a bus?

4. What do you do at break-times and lunch-times?

5. What is your best subject?
   How do you know you're good at it?

6. What is your worst subject?
   How do you know you're not good at it?

7. Do you want to go to university?
   Why? (Why not?)
   Do you know anyone who has been to university?

8. What would you change about the school if you had the chance?

    © IQEA – *Collecting Information for School Improvement*

Interview schedule on teaching and learning issues for disenchanted Y10 pupils

Purpose of instrument

- to determine the orientation to work of disenchanted students;

- to determine factors affecting this orientation;

- to determine the views of disenchanted students on effective lessons and effective teachers.

Advice on administration

As with previous instruments in this section, this schedule can be administered to groups with various orientations to work and ability levels, as assessed by members of staff. If it is used in this way then it is also advisable to interview a control group.

It is best to interview students individually. The interview will take about 20 minutes. It should be administered by someone who doesn't teach in the school, in a quiet area away from the everyday noise of school business.

Some comments on findings

Many of the reasons given by Year 10 students for liking or not liking school relate to teaching and learning in the classroom. More able students rely less on teachers' comments and more on their own self-assessment to judge how hard they are working. Students deemed by staff to show poor work effort are generally aware of their reputations, but claim to be actively working to improve them.

All types of Year 10 students emphasise the importance of understanding work and of the quality of explanation and help offered by teachers. The personal qualities of teachers are also important to all groups. Teaching style and methods are more important elements for the less able students than they are for the more able in assessing the quality of teaching and teachers.

Changes in school tend to concentrate in Year 10 on perceived injustices in the school rules.

Interview schedule on teaching and learning issues for disenchanted Y10 pupils

1. Do you like school?
   Why? Why not?

2. Would you say you worked hard in school?
   How do you know?

3. Have you always been like this?
   When and why did you change?

4. What is your favourite lesson?
   What's good about it?
   What does the teacher do in it?
   What do you do?

5. What is your least favourite lesson?
   What's bad about it?
   What does the teacher do in it?
   What do you do?

6. Without naming him or her, tell me about your favourite teacher of all time.
   What's special about them?
   How did they teach?

7. What would you change about this school if you had the chance, in particular to help you learn more easily?

Interview schedule on motivation of streamed pupils in the middle band

Purpose of instrument

- to determine the orientation to school of students in a middle streamed band;
- to determine their orientation to work;
- to determine their academic aspirations.

Advice on administration

Mixed-gender or single-sex groups of up to four students can be interviewed. Each student should be given an opportunity to answer each question. Interviews take up to 25 minutes, so some 14 groups could be interviewed in a normal school-day. Interviews should be administered by someone who does not teach the group. Because the interviews are quite long, they should be administered in a quiet area where disturbances are unlikely.

Some comments on findings

The middle band in a three-stream year-group is likely to have a wide range of abilities within it. Students were aware of this range. Few appeared to struggle academically. There were frequent bouts of misbehaviour in class, caused in part by student boredom and in part by the teachers' inability to cater for the whole range of ability.

Those interviewed were equally split between those who aspired to move into the higher band and those who were content to stay where they were, with little perceived threat of dropping into the lower stream. Those aspiring to move upward felt there was little chance of so doing, and felt frustrated by factors beyond their control – the disruptive behaviour of other students, and the shortcomings of some of the teachers. Hence the whole of the middle stream was afflicted by apathy and underachievement.

Interview schedule on motivation of streamed pupils in the middle band

1. Do you like school?

2. What do you like most about school?

3. Do you find the work in the middle band easy or difficult?

4. Do you always try your best in class?

5. How do you feel about being in the middle band?

6. Would you like to be in the higher band?

7. What do you think your chances are of moving into the higher band?

Observation schedule on pupil motivation and teacher behaviour
Questionnaire on pupil motivation and teacher behaviour

(derived from the work of Marzano, R. J. *et al.* (1992) 'Dimensions of Learning', *Teacher's Manual*. Aurora: ASCD/McREL).

Purpose of instrument:

- to determine the incidence of motivational teaching strategies used by a teacher in the course of a lesson;

- to determine the extent to which an individual teacher displays motivational behaviours both in and out of class.

Advice on administration

These two schedules should provide complementary data on the same teacher. The observation should be undertaken for the whole of a lesson, and so requires the observer to have a clear view of the teacher at all times. Each instance of a behaviour in the schedule should be noted. It is also possible to chart every teacher-student interaction for a short period, in order that motivational behaviours as a percentage of all behaviours can be calculated. Teachers will be interested in some instant feedback at the end of the lesson.

The questionnaire can be completed at the teacher's leisure, and takes about 20 minutes to complete. It is also a heuristic device, identifying behaviours which have been found to be effective in motivating students and enhancing staff-student relationships.

Some comments on findings

Teachers are often surprised at the number of motivational strategies they already employ, but are also surprised by the nature of some of the strategies they never use. For example, few teachers organise short breaks during lessons where students can move about. Few secondary teachers are aware of their students' birthdays.

Observation schedule on pupil motivation and teacher behaviour

School: Date: Lesson:

(Teacher) Behaviour	Instances
Called pupils by first names as they entered class	
Achieved eye contact with pupils during lesson	
Used humour	
Moved around class and approached all pupils	
Attributed ownership of ideas to initiating pupils	
Responded positively to incorrect answers, identifying correct parts	
Restated questions	
Allowed thinking time	
Rephrased questions	
Gave hints, clues	
Got pupils to restate answers	
Provided answers, asking pupils to restate in own words/ give other examples	
Discouraged pupil-pupil verbal abuse	
Allowed short breaks where pupils moved about	
Organised break when pupils' energy waned	
Conveyed sense of enthusiasm in presentation of task	
Used anecdotes, asides relating to task	
Attributed pupils' successes to their efforts	
Specified what pupils did to achieve success	
Specified expected pupil performance on tasks	
Derived from Marzano *et al.* (1992) 'Dimensions of Learning', *Teacher's Manual*. Aurora : ASCD/McREL.	

Questionnaire on pupil motivation and teacher behaviour

School: **Date:**   **Curriculum area:**

Please circle appropriate answer

1. Do you talk informally with pupils about their interests
   - (a) before lessons? — YES NO
   - (b) during lessons? — YES NO
   - (c) after lessons? — YES NO

2. Do you greet pupils
   - (a) in school? — YES NO
   - (b) outside of school? — YES NO

3. Do you single out a few pupils each day at school locations outside the classroom and talk to them?
   (Please specify locations) — YES NO

4. Are you aware of important events in pupils' lives (like their birthdays)? — YES NO

5. Do you comment on them? — YES NO

6. Do you mentally review classes each day, anticipating likely academic or behavioural problems? — YES NO

7. Do you have positive as well as negative expectations of children with such problems? — YES NO

8. Do you provide opportunities for cooperative learning? — YES NO

9. Do you set tasks involving gathering of information away from desks? — YES NO

10. Do you arrange groupwork? — YES NO

11. Do you allow pupils any say in classroom layout? — YES NO

12. Do you encourage pupils to identify anything annoying them? — YES NO

13. Are there clear rules in the classroom about
    (a) beginning class? YES NO
    (b) use of classroom areas? YES NO
    (c) ending class? YES NO
    (d) interrupting? YES NO
    (e) work requirements? YES NO
    (f) physical safety? YES NO

14. Have you discussed the rationale behind these rules with pupils? YES NO

15. Have you ever changed a rule, for example because of variable situations? YES NO
    (Please specify occasions)

16. Do you enforce these rules consistently? YES NO

17. Have you stressed your concern for pupils' safety and well-being? YES NO

18. Have you ever had occasion to talk to a pupil who has threatened or teased another pupil? YES NO

19. Did you or someone else talk to the pupil's parents? YES NO

20. Have you any procedures in class for inducting new pupils? YES NO
    (Please specify these procedures)

21. Have you found out your pupils' interests and goals relating to your curriculum area? YES NO

22. Do you encourage pupils to generate their own tasks? YES NO

23. Do you encourage pupils to bring in personal items related to topics? YES NO

24. Do you ever break complex tasks into smaller steps? YES NO

Derived from Marzano *et al.* (1992) 'Dimensions of Learning', *Teacher's Manual*. Aurora: ASCD/McREL.

Interview schedule for pupil views on classroom order

Purpose of instrument

- to determine student views on the school's discipline policy;
- to determine students' views on the best ways of dealing with disruptive behaviour.

Advice on administration

This schedule could be administered to a cross-section of students which included a group deemed by staff to be disruptive. Alternatively, it could be administered solely to disruptive students. Because of the sensitivity of some of the questions, it should be administered in each case to individual students by an adult not known to them. The interviews take up to 25 minutes, so 14 students can be interviewed in the course of a school-day. Interviews should take place in a quiet area where disturbances or eavesdropping are unlikely.

Some comments on findings

Students deemed to be disruptive by staff are usually aware that they are disruptive. They are usually boys. Most disrupt in reaction to the context or learning environment in which they find themselves. The stimulus for much of the behaviour is a 'boring' lesson, which students define variously as lessons that are difficult to understand, lessons with a large element of writing, or with little practical work. Fewer disrupt because they enjoy it or because other students are to blame for their disruption. Disruptive behaviour consists largely of talking in class.

Disruptive students are often content that the prevailing system of sanctions is adequate when it is applied justly and consistently. They tend, however, to play down the impact of these sanctions upon their own behaviour, and claim that the quality relationship they have with at least one member of staff is considerably more important in reducing their disruptive behaviour.

Interview schedule for pupil views on classroom order

Y8   **Y9**   **Y10**   **Boy**   **Girl**

1. Do you ever misbehave in class?
   Why?

2. What do you think causes lessons to be disrupted?

3. What kind of pupils cause disruption?

4. What should a teacher do about class disruption?

5. What shouldn't a teacher do?

6. Is there ever rowdy or bad behaviour outside the classroom?
   Where?

7. What should teachers do about it?

8. What shouldn't a teacher do?

9. Which classroom rules do you remember?

10. How do you feel about the rules of classroom conduct?

11. Do you agree with the school rules about behaviour?

© IQEA – *Collecting Information for School Improvement*

Base-line assessment and evaluation

Introduction

IQEA project schools have been rightly concerned about the worth of diverting valuable resources into school improvement projects. They have also wanted to collect evidence that improvement initiatives have in fact worked. More recently, perhaps in the light of current government initiatives, the schools have shown an interest in collecting quantitative as well as qualitative data to aid their evaluations.

Types of information required have included:

- knowledge levels before and at the end of an improvement project;
- audits of effective teaching;
- evaluations of teaching;
- evaluations of organisational arrangements in schools;
- evaluations of departmental and school initiatives;
- checklists for use in the selection of education personnel.

Contents of section

Pupil questionnaire: Spain

Observation schedule relating to features of effective teaching

Pre-lesson questionnaire: pupils

Post-lesson interview schedule: pupils

Post-lesson questionnaire: teachers

Interview schedule for pupils on teacher strategies and learning outcomes

Interview schedule for Y10 pupils' views on the value of Y10 exams

✓ Classroom layout and seating questionnaire

Pupil interview schedule on teaching of fractions

Pupil interview schedule on Eurocentre

Staff interview schedule: action planning for evaluation

Staff interview schedule: evaluation and action planning

Checklist for selection of education personnel

Pupil questionnaire: Spain

Purpose of instrument

- to determine levels of students' knowledge about Spain;

- to establish a group base-line score prior to entry into a project;

- to enable the value added by the project to be measured.

Advice on administration

The questionnaire should be administered prior to students' entry into a project. In this instance the project involved exposure to activities in a Eurocentre specially created by the school to enhance the teaching of Modern Languages. Depending on individual students' knowledge of Spain, the questionnaire can take between 5 and 25 minutes to complete.

The questionnaires of each teaching group involved in the project should be marked separately, and an average number of responses per student should be calculated. It may be possible, for example where Spanish is an optional subject, to have a control group which is not exposed to the Eurocentre. Only manifestly outrageous responses should not be counted. Certain key responses should also be noted, for example what percentage of the group knew that pesetas were the currency of Spain, what percentage identified paella as a Spanish food or what percentage identified Madrid as a Spanish city? The number of different responses per question is also a useful indicator.

Staff should agree on the appropriate time-span before students are re-tested on their knowledge. Students should be given the same questionnaire, and it should be marked in the same way.

Some comments on findings

Six teaching groups were surveyed. Numbers of average responses per group member rose from about 10 in the pre-project test to about 15 post-project. Percentages of students in the pre-test knowing that pesetas were the main currency ranged from 43% in one group to 100% in another – in the post-test the range was 70% to 100%. The range identifying paella as a Spanish food in the pre-test was 0% to 61%, in the post-test 7% to 58%. Madrid was identified by a range of 21% to 89% in the pre-test, by 17% to 92% in the post-test.

Identical questions can be used to test knowledge of other cultures.

Pupil questionnaire: Spain

Please answer these questions about Spain as fully as you can.

Class: **Boy/Girl (circle the right one)**

1. Which foods are eaten in Spain?

2. What do they drink in Spain?

3. What money is used in Spain?

4. What Spanish cities and towns can you name?

5. Which famous Spanish people (dead or alive) can you name?

6. What do people do in their spare time in Spain?

7. In what ways do the Spanish earn money from abroad?

Observation schedule relating to features of effective teaching

(derived from various texts – see Schedule for details)

Purpose of instrument

- to provide an audit of features relating to effective teaching;

- to provide a focus for discussion between staff;

- to provide comparative data, before and after a period of training or induction.

Advice on administration

This schedule can be used by teacher trainers, teacher appraisers or by heads of department seeking to identify good practice. The observer should have a clear view of the teacher at all times. While the features are organised in alphabetical order, the observers will need to acquaint themselves with the schedule before any observation. The schedule allows for the incidence of particular features to be identified in a lesson, but colleagues may be as interested in the range of features employed. Plotting every interaction between students and teacher can be exhausting; merely noting that a particular feature occurs in a lesson is less taxing.

Observations can take place before and after a particular period of training and induction has taken place. Teacher trainers, for example, may wish to observe one of their students during their first lesson, and then later on in the practice in order to discuss progress and possible future action. Head teachers in primary schools might use the schedule in observing a newly-qualified teacher in their first term, and again at the end of their first year. Teacher appraisers can use the data from the observation as a focus for a discussion about effective teaching.

Some comments on findings

Teachers may be surprised at how many of the features already appear in their teaching. They may also be surprised at the incidence of some of them. Certain identified features of effective teaching, for example organising short breaks when students' energies wane, may also come as a surprise.

Observation schedule relating to features of effective teaching

An effective teacher:	
achieves eye contact with pupils during lessons	
allows pupil practice after each learning step	
allows pupils thinking time	
allows short breaks where pupils move about	
asks a large number of questions	
attributes ownership of ideas to initiating pupils	
attributes pupils' successes to their efforts	
avoids digressions/ambiguous phrases	
calls pupils by first names	
checks for pupil understanding	
conveys sense of enthusiasm in presentation of tasks	
discourages pupil-pupil verbal abuse	
gets high percentage of correct answers from pupils	
gets pupils to restate answers	
gives clear/detailed instructions/explanations	
gives concrete, varied examples	
gives hints, clues	
gives moderate amount of praise	
gives short review of previous learning	
guides pupils during initial practice	
has brief contacts with individual pupils (maximum 30 seconds)	
has pupils asking questions/initiating verbal interactions	

highlights main points of lesson	
is knowledgeable about subject matter	
monitors pupils' work when necessary	
moves around class and approaches all pupils	
obtains responses from all pupils	
organises break when pupils' energy wanes	
organises short transitions between activities	
presents new material in short steps	
provides answers, asking pupils to restate in own words/ give other examples	
provides systematic feedback/corrections	
rephrases questions	
responds positively to incorrect answers, identifying correct parts	
restates questions	
specifies expected pupil performance on tasks	
specifies what pupils did to achieve success	
teaches with pace	
uses anecdotes, asides relating to task	
uses humour	

Derived from:

Brophy, J. and Good, T. L. (1991) 'Teacher behavior and student achievement', in (ed.) Wittrock, M. C. *Handbook of Research on Teaching*, 2nd edn. p.271. New York: Harper Collins.
Marzano, R. J. *et al.* (1992) 'Dimensions of Learning', *Teacher's Manual*. Aurora: ASCD/McREL.
Rosenshine, B. and Stevens, R. (1986), 'Teaching Functions' in Wittrock, M. C. *op.cit.*

© IQEA – *Collecting Information for School Improvement*

Pre-lesson questionnaire: pupils
Post-lesson interview schedule: pupils
Post-lesson questionnaire: teachers

Purpose of instruments

- to identify features of effective teaching.

Advice on administration

The pre-lesson questionnaire should be distributed to five or six students prior to the lesson which is being observed. Time should be allowed for them to fill in the questionnaire (about three minutes). The observer should be an adult who does not teach the students. Notes should be made on the lesson by the observer, with a view to filling in the post-lesson questionnaire. The observation schedule on effective teaching which appears in this section could also be used. A post-lesson questionnaire should also be completed by the teacher of the lesson. Students should be withdrawn from the lesson ten minutes before the end in order that the observer can administer the post-lesson interview.

There will thus be a variety of views on the same lesson. Students can be selected by staff according to ability, level of motivation or other criteria.

Some comments on findings

Teachers are able to compare their own versions of a lesson with those of an observer and various types of participant. Where the three parties are agreed on the effectiveness of the lesson, key features of the lesson can be identified, and built into future teaching programmes. Similar pointers can be derived from less effective lessons. Students are generally quite perceptive and frank in their comments about teaching.

Pre-lesson questionnaire: pupils

Boy/Girl: **Class:**   **Subject:**   **Date:**
(circle the right one)

Please answer these questions honestly by underlining the most appropriate response. Bring this sheet with you to the interview.

1.   Do you generally look forward to these lessons?

     a. Yes, a lot

     b. Quite a lot

     c. Sometimes

     d. Not much

     e. Not at all

2.   How well do you feel you have progressed in this subject since you started at this school?

     a. A lot

     b. Quite a lot

     c. Reasonably

     d. Not much

     e. Not at all

3.   How hard do you normally try in these lessons?

     a. Very hard

     b. Quite hard

     c. Reasonably

     d. Not very hard

     e. Not at all

          © IQEA – *Collecting Information for School Improvement*

Post-lesson interview schedule: pupils

	Pupil No.	**Pupil No.**	**Pupil No.**	**Pupil No.**
1. Did you enjoy the lesson? 5 = a lot, 1 = very little				
2. What do you think the lesson was about?				
3. Did you ever lose interest/ switch off? When?				
4. About how many times did you contribute to the lesson?				
5. Is this more or less then usual?				
6. What new things did you learn in the lesson?				
7. Was there anything the teacher did to make it easier to learn?				

Post-lesson questionnaire: teachers

Teacher/Observer: **Class:**   **Subject:**   **Date:**

1.   What was the lesson about?

2.   What opportunities were provided for all pupils to contribute?

3.   How many pupils did you identify as having difficulty in understanding the lesson?

4.   How many pupils in the class would you find it difficult to assess whether they understood the lesson or not?

Interview schedule for pupils on teacher strategies and learning outcomes

Purpose of instrument

- to identify students' views of features of effective teaching.

Advice on administration

This particular schedule is probably more useful in interviewing primary-aged students who have the same teacher for most of the day. It can be administered to mixed-gender groups of up to four students, preferably by a member of staff who does not currently teach them. It takes about 20 minutes to administer, and the interviews can be administered in a quiet area close to the classroom.

Groups can be preselected by staff according to such criteria as ability level, orientations to work or by gender.

Some comments on findings

Students will generally isolate one or more of the various activities they may have undertaken during the particular session under review. Teachers should be able to derive from the responses those teaching strategies which were most effective in enhancing the learning of those students being interviewed.

Interview schedule for pupils on teacher strategies and learning outcomes

1. What did you do this morning/afternoon in class?

2. Did you enjoy it?

3. What did you enjoy about it/dislike about it?

4. What did you learn?

5. What did the teacher do to help you learn?

© IQEA – *Collecting Information for School Improvement*

Interview schedule for Y10 pupils' views on the value of Y10 exams

Purpose of instrument

- to assess the impact of Year 10 exams on students;

- to evaluate the support given to students in the exam period.

Advice on administration

Students should ideally be interviewed individually. Interviews take about 20 minutes, so about 18 students could be interviewed during a normal school-day. Students can be chosen according to ability or motivation levels, as perceived by staff. There should be a gender balance in the sample.

Interviews should take place in a quiet area where disturbances are unlikely. They should be administered by an adult who does not teach the students.

Some comments on findings

Boys find the exams harder, but suffer less stress than girls. Where teacher expectations of students' exam performance have been made explicit, students have been able to assess their own performance more realistically. Few male students feel fully prepared for such exams. They tend to turn for help to teachers and parents for help, but not to friends. Information on revision techniques is valued, as is individual feedback on exam performances.

The exams themselves are valued for the experience of sitting formal papers, and for clarifying in students' minds the work requirements to do well. Few, however, have reflected upon their learning techniques.

Interview schedule for Y10 pupils' views on the value of Y10 exams

1. What were the Y10 exams like?
   How did you do?

2. Did you feel well prepared?
   Who helped you?

3. How much extra work did you do in preparation?

4. Were you given any advice on how to revise?
   What did you find most useful?

5. What feedback did you get on your exam performance?
   Was it useful?

6. How do you feel about your chances in the GCSE exams now?

7. Do you think you will change your approach to working, at school or at home?

8. Has it been useful to have exams in Y10?
   Why?

Classroom layout and seating questionnaire

Purpose of instrument

- to determine student views on classroom seating arrangements.

Advice on administration

Questionnaires can be distributed either to individual teaching groups, to whole year-groups or to the whole school. They take up to ten minutes to complete, so could be done in registration periods or at the beginning or end of a taught period.

Some comments on findings

The horseshoe arrangement is generally regarded by students as useful in class discussions, and is seen as easy to police for teachers. Year 10 students feel threatened by the arrangement. The grouping of tables is favoured by Years 10 and 11, but discounted by Years 12 and 13 as peripheral to effective learning.

The system of desks organised in rows helps to define the social order in Year 10 and Year 11 classes, with an almost universally held view that disruptive students sit at the back, workers sit in the middle row, and 'sad people with no friends' sit in the front. Moving disruptive students from the back of the class to the front is likely to disrupt this social order. Year 10 students acknowledge the usefulness of the arrangement in facilitating learning. Again, sixth formers do not rate this system.

With the data provided from the questionnaires, staff may see the need to adjust the seating in a classroom to meet the needs of a particular teaching situation. Given the importance attached by most students as to where they sit, teachers may themselves want some input into the seating arrangements in their classes.

Classroom layout and seating questionnaire

circle your
Year group   **Y7**   **Y8**   **Y9**   **Y10**   **Y11**   **Y12**

(circle the right one)
Male/Female

Think about your lessons over the last-term.

1. Which of the following classroom plans resembles the type of layout you come across most often?
2. Which plan do you think would help you to learn better?
3. Which plan would you prefer to come across?   (please tick below)

	TEACHER	TEACHER	TEACHER
COME ACROSS	☐	☐	☐
HELP YOU TO LEARN	☐	☐	☐
PREFER	☐	☐	☐

Why do you prefer the one you chose?

Do you think it matters where each individual sits in the classroom (front/back/with friends/near the teacher)?   YES/NO
Please give some brief reasons

Pupil interview schedule on teaching of fractions

Purpose of instrument

- to elicit students' evaluation of a particular teaching style.

Advice on administration

Where a particular initiative covers a whole year-group, as this one did, staff may be keen to hear the views of boys and girls in each of the teaching groups. Students should be interviewed in pairs, a boy and a girl from each group. Interviews take about 20 minutes. They should be administered by someone who doesn't teach Maths to the students who are being interviewed. They should take place in a quiet area away from the classroom.

Some comments on findings

The interviews took place after each teaching group had been given tests on fractions before the project started and at the end of the project. It was therefore possible to identify students who had progressed well, and those whose progress had been less dramatic.

The whole class teaching approach was favoured more by pupils who scored above the average for the year-group, and less by those who scored less than the average. The more able experienced few difficulties with the work. The remainder experienced some difficulties, and would have appreciated more teacher time being devoted to coping with these. The more able felt that they had received more teacher attention to their problems with classroom teaching.

In conjunction with the test data, staff were able through the evaluation to modify aspects of the whole class teaching approach to meet the urgent needs expressed by many of the students interviewed.

Pupil interview schedule on teaching of fractions

1. How did you feel about being taught as a class rather than individually?

2. Did you find the work difficult?

3. Would you have liked more time to work on fractions?

4. Which part of the course did you enjoy the most?

5. Which part did you enjoy the least?

6. Did you work better than in normal booklet lessons?
    In what way?

7. What have you learned?

8. How could the course have been better?

9. Did the presence of a teacher-observer have any effect on you or the class?

Pupil interview schedule on Eurocentre

Purpose of instrument

- to elicit students' evaluations of a new curricular initiative;
- to determine levels of knowledge about the initiative from students not yet exposed to it.

Advice on administration

The interviews are short. For those students who have not visited the Eurocentre, interviews lasted about 3 minutes; for those who had visited, they took about 10 minutes. To avoid disruption to lessons, they can be undertaken in the corridor outside a classroom. They should be administered by an adult not involved in the particular initiative.

Some comments on findings

With this particular initiative, students were enthusiastic, and most felt that it had improved their language learning. All felt that it had improved their cultural awareness of the countries featured in the Eurocentre. Students frequently referred to the atmosphere of the centre, which they felt was markedly different from that of a classroom. They enjoyed role-play in the room, and the apparent lack of pressure to learn. A minority of students found the centre threatening, and preferred the security provided by normal learning procedures in the classroom.

Those students who had not used the centre knew little about it, but were curious and interested about what was within.

Pupil interview schedule on Eurocentre

1. Have you been into the Eurocentre?   YES/NO

2. If NO, what do you know about it?

   (a) Would you like to go into it?

   (b) Why?

3. If YES, why did you go in?

   (a) Did you like it?

   (b) Why?

   (c) Do you think it helps you in learning a foreign language?

   (d) How?

   (e) Do you think it helps you to learn about the country?

   (f) How?

   (g) Is it better than an ordinary classroom?

   (h) Why?

Staff interview schedule: action planning for evaluation
Staff interview schedule: evaluation and action planning

Purpose of instruments

- to provide a matrix for teachers to plan an improvement project;
- to provide a matrix for teachers to evaluate an improvement project, and to plan future action

Advice on administration

The documents are intended to provide frameworks for discussion and action at the beginning and end of a particular improvement project. The discussion can be among members of a cross-curricular working party, members of the same department or, in the case of some primary schools, the whole staff.

Clearly there are some groups both inside and outside the school who will be interested in the evaluation of improvement initiatives – staff who have not been involved, students, parents, governors, advisory staff, colleagues in other schools. The matrices provide a skeleton from which a fuller description of the project, and a fuller evaluation, can arise.

Some comments on findings

Staff who have readily engaged in a school improvement project are generally readily able to take part in discussions about the evaluation of the project. To give greater validation to the evaluation process it may be useful to enlist the services of someone who has not been involved in the project, for example a governor or an adviser.

Staff interview schedule: action planning for evaluation

PURPOSE Why are we doing this? Who is it for?	
FOCUS/EMPHASIS What are we looking at?	
CRITERIA FOR JUDGEMENT How will we assess improvement?	
LOCUS Where will the evaluation take place?	
METHODOLOGY How are we going to collect data?	
EVIDENCE/SOURCES Who or what are we going to gather data from?	
REPORTING Who are we going to tell about this? How are we going to tell them?	

Staff interview schedule: evaluation and action planning

PURPOSE Why did we do this evaluation? Who was it for?	
FOCUS/EMPHASIS What did we look at?	
CRITERIA FOR JUDGEMENT How did we assess improvement?	
LOCUS Where did the evaluation take place?	
METHODOLOGY How did we collect data?	
EVIDENCE/SOURCES Who or what did we gather data from?	
REPORTING Who did we tell about this? How did we tell them?	
OUTCOMES What did we find out? Were there any unexpected outcomes?	
ACTION Where do we go from here?	

Checklist for selection of education personnel

Purpose of instrument

- to provide a checklist to be completed by students applying for places on School Centred Initial Teacher Training (SCITT) schemes (or by teachers applying for jobs at a particular school).

Advice on administration

One of our project schools requested an instrument with which it could vet student applicants to its teacher training programme. They requested a schedule specifying some of the qualities and attitudes needed by teachers who worked in IQEA schools.

The schedule can also be used as a vetting device for prospective teachers. School selection bodies, including governors, decide on the particular profile of student or teacher they are looking for to work in their school, distribute the schedule to the candidates, and compare the completed schedules with their own preferred one.

Some comments on findings

Students and teachers who are familiar with IQEA literature will have little difficulty in filling in the appropriate boxes. Schools may want to adapt the schedule to the needs of their own particular school.

The document provides the basis for an interesting discussion during interviews.

Checklist for selection of education personnel

Please respond to the following statements by ticking the appropriate box. Thank you for your time.

I am a mentor/student. (please delete as appropriate)

	Strongly agree	Mildly agree	Mildly disagree	Strongly disagree
1. Teachers plan best collaboratively.				
2. I would have no reservations in this school about asking for more resources or teaching materials if I felt I needed them.				
3. Teachers should negotiate with pupils about work to be done.				
4. Teachers should help each other with their teaching through classroom observation.				
5. Group INSET sessions are the most effective.				
6. Senior management teams are important in effective classroom teaching.				
7. Pupil feedback is important in improving teaching.				
8. Pupils should be consulted on classroom rules, layout and displays.				
9. Pupils should be able to cope in lessons.				
10. There are pupils it is difficult to get on with.				
11. Disruptive pupils are best dealt with outside the classroom.				
12. Knowledge of pupils' lives outside school is vital to good teaching.				
13. Teachers should review their classes at the start of each day for possible behavioural and learning problems.				
14. Work targets should be set for individual pupils.				
15. Schemes of work should be strictly adhered to.				
16. Pupils should be involved in marking and assessing work.				
17. Class teaching is more effective than teaching different groups in the classroom.				
18. School uniform is a good way of instilling discipline.				
19. Teachers should take part in action research to improve their teaching.				
20. I have something to contribute to the development of my colleagues' teaching.				
21. I read the front part of the TES regularly.				
22. Once I've trained I doubt whether I'll change my teaching much.				
23. It's inevitable that boys get more attention than girls in class.				

Reading

Introduction

Some of the IQEA schools have been concerned about levels of literacy among their students, and have embarked upon improvement projects to raise those levels. Schools have been keen to plot the base-line from which the project starts, and to evaluate any strategies used to try to improve reading levels. Such activity has, of course, been undertaken hand-in-hand with a use of the wide range of reading tests available.

Research attention in IQEA schools has focused on:

- students' reading habits;

- the identification of good practice to develop reading in the classroom;

- evaluations of various classroom strategies used to encourage reading.

Contents of section

Questionnaire on reading habits of secondary pupils

Reading audit – infants' school

Evaluation of teaching strategies used by staff to improve reading in Year 7

Questionnaire on reading habits of secondary pupils

Purpose of instrument

- to determine the kinds of material read by secondary students;

- to determine reasons why students dislike reading;

- to determine some of the ways in which a school could encourage students to read more.

Advice on administration

The questionnaire can be given to whole teaching groups, whole year-groups, whole schools or to groups identified by staff, for example those with poor scores on standardised reading tests. The questionnaire takes up to 20 minutes to complete, and could be completed during a registration period or at the beginning or end of a taught lesson.

Some comments on findings

The percentage of students who admit that they like reading is likely to decline after Year 7, and drop fairly dramatically in Year 9. More boys than girls dislike reading. Adventure, crime and horror books feature prominently in the choice of reading materials for both genders. Magazines and newspapers are also read by large proportions of both. The percentage of those students able to quote the title of the last book they read also declines after Year 7. Students in Years 7 and 8 suggest an increase in the amount of reading material in the library, Year 9 students suggest an increase in the quality of material available.

Students who do not like reading say it is boring. Preferred activities for boys include doing sport and playing computer games, and both genders go out or watch television in Year 9. Magazines and newspapers are occasionally read by both, and both would like more magazines in the library.

Questionnaire on reading habits of secondary pupils

Answer as fully as you can.

1. Do you like reading?   YES   NO   (circle answer)

If YES, carry on to *Question 2*.
If NO, go to *Question 6*.

2. What kind of books do you enjoy reading?
   (Crime? Romance? Sport? Others?)

3. What other kinds of reading material do you like?
   (Magazines? Newspapers? Others?)

4. What was the last thing you read?

5. How could the school improve its library?

If you answered NO to Question 1, start here.

6. Why don't you like reading?

7. What do you like doing in your spare time?

8. Do you ever look at printed materials?
   (Newspapers? Programmes? Others?)

9. What would you like to read in school?

Thank you for taking the time to fill in this questionnaire.

Reading audit – infants' school

Purpose of instrument

- to provide a matrix to chart good classroom practice relating to encouraging students to read.

Advice on administration

The matrix can be filled in by a curriculum coordinator, head teacher or, indeed, any member of staff. The list is accumulative, so observers should start with a blank sheet. Features of the classroom which encourage students to read can be added as the observer moves from classroom to classroom. The matrix lists the features identified in one school.

In this way the good practice already existing in the school can be logged. The completed matrix provides the basis for a staff discussion on good practice, and enables curriculum coordinators to highlight where development and training may need to be done.

Some comments on findings

There is often a wide range of good practice in schools, but certain aspects may be limited only to a few classrooms. The staff discussion enables individual teachers to explain and justify these aspects to members of staff who do not use them.

Reading audit – Infants' school

Accumulative list   **Classes visited**

Observed	1	2	3	4	5	6	7	8	9	10
Names/labels										
Instructions										
Questions										
Alphabet										
Phonic display										
Word lists										
Book display										
Books available										
Reading scheme										
AVA work/games										
Dictionaries										
Lesson using book										

Evaluation of teaching strategies used by staff to improve reading in Year 7

Purpose of instrument

- to determine the effectiveness of various teaching strategies used in the classroom to improve reading.

Advice on administration

The questionnaire should be distributed to all teaching staff. It takes about 20 minutes to complete.

The strategies listed in the table were those agreed by the staff of one school. Staff were at liberty to choose one or more of the strategies to integrate into their teaching. Schools may, of course, wish to amend the list.

Some comments on findings

A collation of the data from the completed questionnaires provides the basis for an interesting staff discussion about the comparative effectiveness of the strategies tried. Coordinators will wish to generalise the use of any strategies which have proved effective for a number of staff.

Evaluation of teaching strategies used by staff to improve reading in Year 7

I am in the _____ Department.

1. Which of the following strategies did you use in your lessons? How often did you use them?

Strategy	Used? (please tick)	How often?
Introducing 'key words'		
Teacher reads to pupils		
Reading level of materials assessed		
School library used		
Paired reading organised		
Reading Support Programme		
Reading materials taken home		
Reading for comprehension		
Paired spellings		
Students read aloud in class		

2. Describe briefly how you integrated the strategy/strategies into your lessons.

3.   Were there any difficulties in integrating the strategies?
     Was there any support the school could have provided?

4.   Did the strategy/strategies improve the reading of your Year 7 students?
     How do you know?

5.   Will you continue to use the strategy/strategies in future lessons?
     Why?/Why not?

Index